Pavilion

Pavilion
Deborah Tyler-Bennett

Published 2010 by
Smokestack Books
PO Box 408, Middlesbrough TS5 6WA
e-mail : info@smokestack-books.co.uk
www.smokestack-books.co.uk

Pavilion
Deborah Tyler-Bennett
Copyright 2010, Deborah Tyler-Bennett all rights reserved
Cover image: Rex Whistler, 'HRH The Prince Regent Awakening the Spirit of Brighton', photograph reproduced with the kind permission of The Royal Pavilion and Museums (Brighton and Hove)

Printed by
EPW Print & Design Ltd

ISBN 978-0-9560341-5-1
Smokestack Books gratefully
acknowledges the support of
Arts Council England

LOTTERY FUNDED

Smokestack Books is
represented by Inpress Ltd
www.inpressbooks.co.uk

For Martyn, my ideal husband

Acknowledgments

Some of these poems previously appeared in the following publications: *Bard, The Black Mountain Review* (Northern Ireland), *A Cornish Assembly* (Boho Press), *Chanticleer, Cauldron, Erratica, The International Notebook of Poetry, Lamport Court, The New Writer, Poetry Cornwall, Poetry Monthly, Poetry Nottingham International, Poetry Scotland, Poets Anonymous, Read the Music, The Slab, Speaking English: Poems for John Lucas,* (Five Leaves), *Staple, The Trick of Watching* (Leicestershire Open Museums) and *The White Car* (Ragged Raven Press).

Thanks are due to the many poets, friends, and listeners who have been supportive of my work over the years, including: Martyn Bennett, my parents, Jack and Doris Tyler, and sister, Rachel, Lora Redman and her family, Mike Bartholomew Biggs and Nancy Mattson, Jack Yates, John Lucas, Gill Spraggs, Mark Goodwin, Nikki Clayton, Jonathan Taylor, Chris Jones, Alan Joyce, Lisa Webb, Sally Evans, Richard Livermore, Malcolm Carson, Liz Cooper and the late Mary Cooper, my creative writing students, all at *Rhymes and Wine* Loughborough, Tony Lewis-Jones, Sam Gilliland, Stig Evans, Peter and Jill Seddon, Les Merton, John Gallas, Anne Stewart, Lidia Vianu and her Romanian translators. Thanks also to the dandy spirit of the elegantly-dressed everywhere, especially Duggie Fields, and to the city and people of Brighton, both continuing sources of pleasure and inspiration.

Contents

Brighton Poems
- 9 West Pier Serenade
- 10 Greene-Land
- 11 Carry on at Your Convenience
- 12 The Brighton Mystery
- 13 Peep Show
- 14 Tonight and Every Night
- 15 Under Suspicion
- 16 Artist
- 17 Mr Saturday Night
- 18 Good Time Girl
- 19 Less than Sod All
- 21 Viewed from Jack Vettriano's Pier
- 22 Photo Romance – Seaside Special
- 24 Glitter-Guns and Gangstas
- 25 Penny Falls
- 30 Sugar Town
- 32 The Arctic Monkeys Sing His Soundtrack
- 34 Someone for the Weekend
- 35 Time at the Patrick Hamilton
- 37 Heist
- 40 The Adventures of Jane
- 42 Spiv
- 43 Gin and 'It Girls'
- 44 Rampage at Burgess Hill
- 46 State Funeral
- 48 Let's Not Stick Around for This
- 50 Escapologists
- 52 Regent
- 53 Jimmy and Steph
- 54 Permanent Crease
- 56 We Are (Still) the Mods

Dandies
59 Self Portrait of the Artist as Tank Commander
60 The Boy with Harold Steptoe's Despair
61 'Let Me Tell You the Story of My Life...'
62 Teds and Aristos
63 Good Time Girl II: Vanitini
64 River Song
66 Links
67 Monsieur Worth
68 Dan Dare and the Mansfield Aliens
69 Dan Dare's Living Daylights
70 Dan Dare and the Vanished Years
72 Montague Burton: Definitely a Ladies' Man
73 Bread and Cakes
74 No Man
75 Regular
76 Portrait of Mr ...
78 Flaneur

Brighton Poems

West Pier Serenade

There's a dance going on in the dark above our heads,
men pressing women against laundered suits,
a girl's surprised to find her older partner dances
better than boys, a woman leaves imprinted lips
staining the bar-tender's milky cheek.

Above us, the burned-out Pier against evening's
Guinness-black curtain, where feet shuffle in rhythm
(a few toes getting stepped on), and maybe this
close stepping's what we're made for,
hands tight against gabardine or georgette clad backs.
It may be the sea, or the dancers' suggestive whispering:
'At last, at last, at last …'

Above our heads, pier-bones lost to night,
where phantoms clutch each other.
Only the sea? Or a woman breathing to her partner,
before kissing him: 'I wish tonight would last,
would last … would last …'

Greene-Land

Brighton-Rock-facades bear
evening's peeling sunburn,
front slaying grounds where Pinkie,
Spicer, Cubitt rent.

Man ghosting balcony
(small hotel or private apartment
lost to dark's full dinner-dress)
echoing brittle century.

Pinkie's nemesis, Colleoni,
imbibing night's legitimate air.
Gangster's glacé eyes fix our backs,
look up – only red-tipped fag.

Further on, improbable hoodlum
sports noir-trilby, car's unsteady light
revealing gun (for sale?) Spots us. Hands piece
driver-wards. Stalks off. No words.

Car shadows.
Faster we go
grateful for neon windows,
courting couples making him turn away.

Just escaping Pinkie's day,
sour as hot breathing on the face.

Quitting balcony, Colleoni
awaits report from hired guns.

Carry On at Your Convenience

for John Lucas

Old man huddled on the Palace Pier, sloped as a displaced beach-hut.
Belonging more to the burnt-out West Pier, he hugs a *Waitrose* bag
filled with rat-eared holiday brochures promising Pinewood sets
of azure skies and gull-white hulls.
                                     He fidgets them, revealing
copies of *Gramophone*. Signs behind him read:
NON-DESIGNER SUNGLASSES/ NON-DESIGNER PRICES.
Rough laughs break against his head, like cinema crowds
hooting at Charles Hawtrey, Bernard Bresslaw,
Barbara Windsor.

Later, he pads *The Victoria Bar*, adrift on splitting trainers.
Shifts, clawing the bag, as customers
(dead-spits of Hattie, Kenneth, Joan) holiday round him,
as staff mop spillages.

If this was 'Carry-On', the barmaid would lean enormous boobs
towards some weedy punter, asking innocently if he
liked the view, barmen sporting names like Widdle,
Endaway, and Bigger endlessly dropping pints.
The old man's magazine? *Wink*
or *Titbits*, not *Gramophone* (unless someone
was to ask did he: 'Buy it for the horn section?')

Piped over the bar, Hollywood assaults his ears:
'Move Over Darling' … 'Secret Love' …
Doris Day holding notes longer than a *Brighton Promette's* legs,
honeyed as the promise of bleached hair.

As he steps out, catch Sid James's randy laugh
undercutting Hollywood's touch of mink.

The Brighton Mystery

Dripping dusky verdigris,
West Pier emerges – last year's discarded Christmas tree.
Interior rain-forest,
armed branches dripping, lowest
in sea. Sun bakes pebbles, old columns
(monster nails commissioned,
then abandoned) stand stark.
Later, it's smothered in dark
until the fortune-teller's kiosk hovers, white
ghost of Max Miller's suit.
Catch phosphor outlines of a pier that's whole again
waves echo applause like rain,
hinting a performance to which we're uninvited,
come morning, whole scene righted,
West Pier skeletal, waiting for night.
Strung lights,
hint at decline …
                        Joke with long forgotten punch-line.

Peep Show

Past stair-wells' shattered lids and inner-eyes
lie secretive closed rooms,
their sobs and sighs.

Door opening – bald occupant haloed
as a waitress hands a glass of Chardonnay,
then all's clammed shut.

From upper-levels torn white papers faint,
dropping at our feet.
child cascading them chuckles to see her boats

float…

voice chivvying floor to floor, paper's
delicate flakes glare against carpet.

Somewhere, waves flash
hard, pristine, wondrous
as the Pier's fixed mirror-ball.

Tonight and Every Night

During two hours drinking, chatting
to a dedicated follower of fashion, a drunk's
careered in and out of reception three times,
        slammed three times into the desk,
asked three times: 'This my hotel?' Unstirred receptionist
takes the lad's mobile, phones his friend:
Right hotel, lost room-key.
Single-stag buys the hen-party a round, sleeps, wakes, asks:
'Why'm'I sitting here with you?' Bare-
arsed, a rubber-suited man circles the door,
'that'll chafe in this heat', our companion grins.
Bride-to-be in sexy frock and Fireman's helmet
clambers stairs, telling mates about a man she met:
'Might look him up on the way home. It don't mean anything,
he were a right laugh.' Four blokes arrive in search of beds,
everything's booked. Beet-faced man whines:
'No hot water, no milk, wrong coffee,
burst tea-bags' … Bare-arse stalks to his rest, John Wayne style.

Earlier, we'd moved because a loud man shoved another
off the slots: 'I've got cash in that mate', all he said.
Now, his ash-faced girlfriend clatters, her arm in his vice,
his words bitten: 'We're going out, right?'
Earlier, she'd left the bar, gone to bed.

They push through open doors, her green eyes
wetter than the ocean-view.

Under Suspicion

Nautilus-balustrades, initialled *H.N.* for
Hotel Norfolk, staircase's grandeur muted
by a corporate image. Where it should sweep,
the metal train's truncated by fire-doors -
shrunk, a Hartnell gown in charity-shop window.

What should be elegant's squiggled hastily
in clashing ochre, fuchsia, kingfisher,
uniform-carpets attack the eye.

Through open doors, darkening road, sea, sky …

And is it me, or do past denizens roam blocked-
off corridors? The later it gets, the more they're sensed,
until the sea's longing-suggestions become feet
deliberately en-route to wrong rooms, voices hustling,
shifty footfalls of detectives out to catch men
and women in unexpected beds.

Walking towards us, the Dandy in dark glasses
ghost of a man who wanted to get caught,
holding out slender wrists. Porcelain cuff-links
bearing legends: 'Guilty' and 'Not Guilty'.
'Which is it, do you think?' He asks

gentle voice echoing waves.

Artist

Around him waltz rouged women and louche
men, or Spivs and Good Time Girls push by his chair,
lobby filling with slit gowns and rented-suits.

He's better dressed than them, *Versace* handkerchief,
gilt 1940s watch, strap fragile as sunglasses
kept on indoors.

Flamed tie (shapely as a red sheath-dress),
face set, hands manicured, walk sloped, as if emerging
from one of the pictures he copies for a living.

Dark glasses making eyes unreadable, he could be
film-noir villain, or victim, delicate fingers
made for circling wine-glass.

Stepping between scarlet and jet
he holds out photographs of favoured images
like Tarot Cards:

Competition dancer, number at his back, gazing
from a balcony... Girl in titanium chiffon
mauling roses... Well-heeled couples paddling.

'Which do you like?' He asks, I point to
the numbered man. Signs the photo's back
hands it to me, fingers trembling.

His voice is full of cases being packed, of clasps snapped shut,
petals dropping, dance-number taken off,
and cast bin-wards,
                full of wine-glasses in undetected corners,
of Flash Harrys and satin-clad honeys, leaning out
from repeating canvases of black, white, crimson.

Mr Saturday Night

He says, my face reflected in his shades:
'Do you know what a Teddy-Boy was?' I
nod. 'Used to be one, but not now – why?
Today it's shaven-heads, so real class fades,
p'raps I should shave mine?' Grey eyes, steel blades,
glinting from behind slipped glasses. 'Should I
streak my hair, wear jeans, give up?' He breathes a sigh
and knows he shouldn't. Dandy who parades
style, ash-bouffant gleams. 'Look at me, who the
fuck wears this stuff anymore?' Gestures down
at winkle-pickers. 'David Dickinson!
That's who they thought I was tonight. Me! …
They're talking bollocks!' Now, his whole frame frowns:
'and who the fuck *is* David Dickinson?'

'I've been to 'Grab a Gran Night'. Hove Town Hall.'
This story he tells twice, tones softly slurred,
speaking as if the picture's slightly blurred:
'I partnered this old bird – God help us all!
Eighty she was… I'm sixty… had a ball …
too old for me… Trapped in her zimmer… whirred
round the floor, took ages. Then it occurred
to me she was just thankful not to fall,
lipstick bled in tram-lines round her mouth.
My fault for going. Look at me now, love,
who wears this anymore? Bollocks, I say.
Everyone shrivels, yeah, our looks go South,
and that fucking cash does us no good …'

Removing sun-glasses he turns away.

Good Time Girl

World's biggest cliché, I know, falling for a shadow-
suited man, whose eyes are always shaded.
Wrong un', crook, alcoholic, always the short-con
for a man who could unhook
bra-clasps without me knowing. Now he's gone
(this time how long?)

Mirrored face stares back,
hair sleek as Betty Boop,
nasturtium lips. In day-dreams I'm light
years younger, slimmer, tanned.
Mirror woman, scornful of her own hand's
hasty packing. *Agent Provocateur*
slip slung in without tissue-paper.
One thing rooting me,
stilettos, the only balance-keepers.
Their grip, an imprint of his grasp.
I totter reception-wards with minimal luggage,
key, excuses.

Fogged face of the man I won't forget burned on
my retina, like the West Pier's negative
after a day of sun.

Less than Sod All

Patient Dublin lilt exploring every possibility,
their friends been in touch, arrived? No?
Well, here's the thing now, could they ring
this number, leave a message? Grand. So
they'll ensure friends know
they arrived? Great, so
will they call when people come? Oh,
and they've to come from Bournemouth, how
long'll that take? Thanks.
Paces multicoloured
carpets in multicoloured
shirt, while his partner settles
in a distant chair –
Says nothing
does nothing
if nothing
was sporting
he'd achieve Olympic gold …

One more thing… How long'll it take to get to Hove?
Thanks, love.
Could she book
dinner? Oh,
joy with the call? No?
Early days.
His partner blends
eerily with the chair –
Silent
unresponsive
if nothing
was stardom
he'd be resurrected
plated-suited
Elvis …

His man's voice drifts reception

over Technicolor yawns of carpet and shirt,
as he does bugger all, sweetest FA
to platinum standard
excelling at nada,
making other men in chairs look active. Flickering in and
so far-out of his matched-shirt's psychedelic happening.

Viewed From Jack Vettriano's Pier

Chisel faced punters, and bored-shitless attendants
suggest dangerous seas caressing pier struts,
ready to turn and smash.
Dodgem blues and yellows paint People's Republics of Brighton,
Blackpool, Scarborough.
                       Not genteel 'coast' this, but 'seaside' where
hotels (lacy eyes once blinking on better times)
host ballroom spies, sex games, and shadow dancers.

Rock-stripy skirts foaming pin-ups' legs,
sun-glasses glamorise tired faces, chilled hearts are
nickels, dimes, tossed at will by movie mobsters.

Love Me or Leave Me echoes over Penny Slots -
Fortune Teller, What the Butler Saw,
and terrifying *Laughing Policeman,*
his drill-throated vocals gull scattering.

Photo Romance - Seaside Special

He must've been good looking once. Tall.
Purpling under grime, elegance dirt-
hidden, that, and the drugs don't work.
Ownerless shadow reeling The Front,
beyond-pissed-self blotting hoardings,
leathers barely supporting
as boots scuff gravel, to travel back
a step
        three forward
  back two
                        tight-rope walking
to accompanying Ska band
jamming atop a transit with 'One Step Beyond' …
Miracle of road negotiation, he gets across.
                                      Ghost
of a smile's ghost,
acknowledging this time, time
hasn't knocked him down.
                          She must've been a looker once. Waiting.
Fuming behind a kiosk,
as daredevil road-cross
repeats –
        Forward two.
Back another.   LUNGE
He hasn't begged, sponged
beer, spoken.
Now, flaps to where she is,
resumed fight broken
only by 'Too Much Too Young.'
He's off again. *Brillo*-pad hair
complicates that half-cut silhouette, *FUN
AT SEALIFE* sliced by slender legs
wobbling down beach-steps.
One forward
        Forward
Back, next high-wire begins.
She slams away.

Other people's dramas, unwinding photo-play,
leave me wondering no one turns to say:
'How do his *Fendi* shades stay
so immaculate?' Fixed, no matter how life sways
and descent more than threatens.

Glitter-Guns and Gangstas

'Hale knew, before he had been in Brighton three hours, that they meant to murder him.' (Graham Greene, *Brighton Rock*)

Pistol pendants, diamanté names: Ryan,
Kev, Wayne, Tricia.
Monkey-metal spelling: 'TURBO',
letters rhinestoned on clutch-bags:
'Gangsta', 'Slapper',
'If you think I'm a bitch, you should see my mother.'
Chandelier earrings against necks of old women
eyeing up Saturday Boys in the Pier Shop:
'Hasn't he a lovely arse, Madge?'
'He has.'

Ruby-glass encrusted bullets, men built like
Tony Soprano sporting dollar signs big
as pickle-jar lids.

Gold teeth, bellies studded silver,
twenty-two sovereign rings on mottled hands,
someone plays the slots freighted with chains.

Here, where life's candy-striped for the weekend,
where men and women giggle like kids
at *Pier-Side Massage, Crack a Crab*,
or *Grand Theft Auto*, where you can kiss and kill
then go for a bag of chips
the child-eyed geezer scans crowds
for the older man he has to slash.

Penny Falls

I Change and Tokens Here

I'm seeing him push money in the slots,
like there's no tomorrow, 2p, 2p, 2p –
you can win fags, a slide of 5ps, knuckle-dusters saying
CHAV and *SLAG*. 10p, 10p, 10p,
win tin-foil watches, bundled tenners, slides of more 10ps,
except you never bloody do – 30p
the claw inches towards *Disney* toys (or *Grizzly* toys)
for the girlfriend, a pair of *Kalvin Clean* shades, that cost
us less than 30p to buy. He's at the change machine again,
then at my window, and can I change a tenner?

'Course I can, it's what I'm here for, love.'

II Anthony

Her booth, a shining casket, Snow White frozen
under a sign for change. Waiting her prince and
who's to say I'm not him? I'm too old, who'm I kidding?
Our eyes meet but she never, ever smiles,
just waits for me to spend my change with other suckers.
She sees me as a tourist, here at weekends, who'm I kidding?
She doesn't look at me at all.
I used to be a teacher, had a car, a mortgage… that'd bore her.
If we ever speak, I'll make up some big story, say
I'm living at *The Grand*, she'll see right through that,
best to say the truth, or nothing… Nothing might be best.

III Barry

Sometimes, I dream the silver sound of them
dropping, as all the machines give it up together,
that girl looks straight through me, in my dream,
as I rush from slot to slot, picking up winnings.

Yesterday, I almost broke *Niagara*, saw the edge-
coins wobble. It's just a laugh, this, passes time,
tonight I'm back at the *Casino* waiting on the real
top-dollar.

IV Denver

Coffee's crap – tastes of sand and water.
Won't complain again. Last time, almost
got me barred, that and using staff washrooms.
Softening, these biscuits are crap as well.
Have to go soon. Other fish to fry. Can't
make this last much longer, they're
giving me that dead eye again, thinking
I'm no better than a tramp: 'Sod off looking,
wankers!' Did I say that out loud?
Christ! It's getting worse.

V Brenda

That one looks alright, beige suit, retro-tie,
hair slicked back, a bit like Bryan Ferry with a squint,
he's been pushing that machine for ages, but stops
to eye me up. He grins, clean teeth.
Shame on you sonny, I'm old enough to be your mum,
but let's not go there, eh? You look the sort that doesn't care,
the boy most likely to, and there again
you've got
        to have
                a bit of fun
                        before it's
                                    painted black –

it's what we're here for.

Sugar Town

Silver wedges, lingerie flittering
like magenta butterflies forced
earthwards by 'up yours' grins.
On the Prom -
schlongs in sarongs,
chicks with dicks,
cocks and frocks.

Lucille Balls, Miss Kitty,
Mis-Take, Lola Lost-My-Little-Willy,
Vera Vibrator. Calves most girls standing here
do nothing but envy.

How come his legs
are so damn long?
Sharon Stone
with value added
throwing Casino-chips
at bad boys' faces,
blonde ambition a visible panty line.

De Niro clones should crowd their route
(ice cream coloured suits,
vanilla, pistachio, *Apricot-Slice*,
or, maybe, *Rocky Road*)
fingering crimson dice
while praying not to fall in love.

Women on the Prom
(including me) chorusing: 'How come
his foxy legs are so damn long?'
Sharon Stone
with value added, peroxide ambition's
VPL casting Casino-
chips at bad boy faces.

A made man clutches ruby dice and prays
dark eyes won't betray
cartoon love-hearts making way
through tongue tied lips -
his hetero-swagger, for the last time, slips.

The Arctic Monkeys Sing his Soundtrack

'You've delivered the vegetables,
now I'm stuck here, on this fucking beach …'

He might add: 'And it's dark, and I'm looking at
a shut Fishing Museum, bolted huts,
lights swinging over couples going home from pubs,
or out to club-land.
And, incidentally mate, not only am I stuck,
having made your shitting delivery,
but I'm wearing a leather-look, fake *Armani*,
squeaky suit, or maybe
it's wearing me.'

(Too tight under arm, crotch, bum).

'That sound? This crappy
mobile someone sold me,
you have to bellow to be heard,
suddenly looks bigger than my hand,
oh, I'm way beyond stressed,
you're breaking up… understand
I DID NOT CHOOSE TO BE HERE!
Wearing sunglasses in the dark,
which, I thought, mistakenly, as it turned out,
would make me look just like a cool bloke in a song.
How wrong was I? How wrong?
I'll tell you … Actually,
like The Monkeys say
the look's all gone "a bit Frank Spencer"…'

His winded words should blow away,
anger tightening that plastic suit,
if some joker held a mirror up
he'd be facing desperation
in the dark, in those 'imitation
of an imitation' shades,

things go tits up, loco, turbo,
more than just a bit Pete Tong
and it's all gone
as The Monkeys say
come on, you know the song.

Someone for the Weekend

for Rachel

Copied Jack Vettriano, where the man's
gazing at the woman's black-panty clad arse,
speculatively, appreciatively,
even vacantly…
Breathing cigarette smoke between thighs
as if she's a plastic coffee-table in female form.
So seedy it makes me smile.
Could he be more of a wide boy?
Maybe she asked: 'Do that thing with the smoke.'
Perhaps she's just a plastic coffee-table in female form.

Like him, I'm black-panty gazing but
they're displayed on a shop front
with other Vettriano gamesters
(painted by less celebrity Jack-the-Lads).
As the shop owner emerges I almost say: 'Think she asked
for that thing with the smoke?'

Know how sometimes you don't look hard enough
gasping at what it's unbelievable you missed?
This is one of those.
Stepping from Vettriano's
world rather than a shop –
Cobalt suited, link wearing,
gold chain bearing,
bullet-headed B-movie man,
his picture ricochets.

'It's the smartest
one that. Others inside,
prices good, no joke.
I only open weekends.'

Him melting back inside the shop, like smoke.

Time at The Patrick Hamilton

'We've come on holiday by mistake... We're not from London.'
(*Withnail and I*)

It never changes. Sign reads OPEN both ways,
hostelries surrounding *Hangover Square*
veered into by moth-balled actors, colonels,
salesmen, occasional passers-by
(primed to swallow lines
from sherry-eyed barmaids, love-
heart lips *Cherry Brandy*).

Pubs, snugs, bars. Loungers,
mugs, thugs, stars, scroungers.

Cast-list predictable, some bloke
slinks down, no one rescues him,
bulk stranded between brogues
and kitten-heels.
Joker half-inches his trilby,
squeezes it on, grimacing.

Whisky, Gin, and Lemon-Bitters:
'ere too long, mixing with quitters.'

Couple, almost dancing.
Slapped, he grabs her wrist,
she challenges pacifying barmen:
'What's eating you? We're not pissed.
Sobriety, a point of view.

Wine bar. Chill Out. Hotel. Club.
Fine Time Experts. Snacks in tubs.

Couple chucked-out, not before
her glass's smashed into a tray of ice,
they'll discover mirrored paradise
a few doors down.

                    It never changes.
Just the pin-ups' hair, their cocktail choice,
just the Landlord's face, but not the lies:
'Do hurry back.' Echoing pubs, snugs, lounges
on multiplying streets under blurred skies.

Heist

'A Dame Worth Dying For...' Frank Miller, Sin City

I Double Indemnity

Poker faced men and guilt-edged women.

Killing each other in downpours,
or driven scheming to lonely places
with names like *Hangman's Bluff, Desolation
Peak, Angel Horizon*. Or sitting apart
in bars like this, *Heist*, décor suitably black,
an ad for *Hired Goons Wanted for Christmas*
at the door, barman looking as though trouble
could enter, kissing you on the lips, leaving
incriminating scarlet, as if some low life punched
you on the jaw.

II The Killers

She considers you, with mantis elegance,
Venus, fly-trapping, she sips a *Metropolitan*
with that 'come here, big-boy' cool
all the patsies fall for.
This is Brighton, could be hell or Hove,
or anywhere night-hawks gather.
Rows of glassware reflect faces
trying each other on for size.
A couple leave together,
doors swing like a movie's penultimate shot.

Crescendo overload as credits roll.
Final close-up: Yellow sign for festive *Hired Goons*,
dropped gardenia on a rain-smeared street.

III The Postman Always

struggles up this stretch, which, it being noir,
can only be one way.
Heist's prison high walls forbid entry until opening hours.
Flambeaux outside. He expects doors to reveal
Lana Turner in a long white robe,
legs set off by pillar-box red heels,
Sidecar clutched in mandarin lacquered nails.

'Come about the hired goon job?'
She pouts, suggesting far from simple plans
and jeopardy yet to come.

The Adventures of Jane

'Just in case I ever go his way again',
she thought. 'I'm never getting caught without slap,
I'll take Vivienne Westwood's advice:
'If in doubt, overdress.'
He'll take one look and 'bang!'
like a pistol being fired.'

Standing in a hotel-foyer, fired
by picture-perfect images, she muses: 'Again,
it's happening again, bang-
out-of-order. My looks'll be a slap
in the face for him. Mustn't really over-dress,
though. Easy does it, best advice.

Aunt Vi said: 'Let me give you some advice,
girl, always dress well, you'll never be fired'.
Don't think it's really over… Dress
needs pressing… stained again …
Only one thing with wearing slap
it marks you'. Outer doors go 'bang'

it's not her cab, just the sea breeze, 'bang'
again, the receptionist's giving out advice
to some geezer on the phone: 'We're slap
on the front, sir.' She smears 'fired
terracotta' lipstick. 'Again'
she thinks, recalling how they rowed over a dress.

'Just a fling, doesn't do to over-dress
it. Ruth Ellis, and Rice-Davies, getting fired-
up over toffs. Am I the same? Again
I'm offering myself some good advice
I'll never take. Like the record said 'bang
bang, he shot me down.' Love's just a slap.

I could leave now, still walk slap
into him. If I'd got on some sloppy overdress
he'd think I'd gone maternal. Fired
terracotta suits me. Bang. Bang.
Who needs advice?
I'm never going to see the guy again.'

Her joke-shop pistol's waiting to be fired,
black letters saying 'BANG!' Advice?
No point. Looks like pulp fiction hits its mark again.

Spiv

Rock Shop: Bacon, egg, sausage, ham, tomato, beans,
dummies, sticks, shells, pebbles, lobster-
platter, winking red…

Sell them anything while they're here.
Watches that'll last the day out if they're lucky,
rhinestones adrift on liquid faces below crackling glass,
time melting as they dance on the front, under bar-lights,
with some girl who'll regret it in the morning.

Plastic pendants at silver prices,
boxed fudge saying: THIS GIFT IS FOR MY FAVOURITE
OLD CODGER/ SLAPPER.
Stags and hens buying wands, light up crowns, and
these bracelets, links softening in sun,
stones that'll get lost among
beach pebbles. Buying them off me in pubs, car-
parks, on the Pier.

I've been known for flogging things less trivial
in the past, may do again, case of watch this space –
flogged promises of time-share,
golden business opportunities,
love,
(that perhaps the biggest crock of all,
false as sugar kippers on a paper plate).

The way her eyes scan mine
for meaningful signs.
While she looks at me to tell her something good,
I hear a bag's zipper pull shut,
my footsteps down carpeted stairs,
heading door-wards, towards another hotel in a distant town.

Gin and 'It Girls.'

for Mum, Dad, and the memory of Maud

'Tumbler full of gin, love, nothing else.
(They know me). Tonic separate.' Waving *Pony* glass,
jet beehive decked with spangled bow,
Carry-on-Cleo eye-shadow,
must be eighty-odd or so.
Hubby slumps. 'Poor old sod!'
She cackles: 'Doesn't know he's here,
chin-up, Lovey, have another beer!'
Friend, hair peachy candy-floss,
takes ages to negotiate steep stairs,
greets me in the loo:
'Must undergo repairs,
after all, don't do
not to wear lippy.'
Smiles, *Pin-Up-Girl-Poppy*.

Suddenly, I'm back with you,
greeting us in *Eastman-Colour* frock,
over eighty, psychedelic jewellery
achieving culture shock,
grinning through orchid lippy.
Then, that paler vision, when you'd gone –
champagne with mourners in your room,
daughter relishing fiesta wardrobe,
gold heels resisting gloom.

Just as quick, I'm stood with her again,
asking if re-figured lips are blotted:
'You were miles away, I hope he's nice,' she scoffs,
pinching hoop earrings. Clotted
cream powder fixed, and off.

In my mind's eye, you join them for a laugh,
army of old *Carry-on-Film* crumpet. Still
ready to cavort with Sid and Babs,
parading Brighton seafront dressed to thrill,
before their paid-up journeys in *Glam Cabs*.

Rampage at Burgess Hill

Calvin Klein y-fronts poking from *Anti-fits*,
mobile gripped in beetroot mitts:
'I'm fucking owed and calling it in,
and on the pissing train, bin
waitin' all morning! You listening?'
Sweat oils his back, glistening
as, phone in pocket,
starts to rocket
up and down carriages, menacing
with push-ups, clutching rails, grimacing
pumps, jumps. Mobile buzzes
and he loses
cool: 'I am shittin' getting off at Burgess Hill,
and you better be there, Phil,
got it? Burgess Hill… They'll taste our rage,
'cos we're goin' rampage.
You better be up for it!'
Stares round, sits,
stretches legs, hoping someone trips,
only a toddler pushes past,
Mum apologetic. At last
(nothing kicking off)
he's up again: 'Toff
and Fat Barry better come, I'm tellin' you,
rampage… Not the type to let things stew.
Owed and collecting. Right?
We're coming in, hold nuts, sit tight,
let's sort it. Righteous. Try
soundin' convinced: I'M ENGLAND 'TILL I DIE!'
Starts to bellow, getting off,
my Sister whispers: 'He's Tim Roth,
in *Made in Britain*',
soon, train's slipping
from Burgess Hill and coming rampage,
revenge on today's debt and outrage.

Pictures form of his bare back's
bruises from previous attack –
Perfect impression of a *K-Swiss* on young skin,
an iron's imprint, reddening.

State Funeral

At *British Swearing Awards*, hands down,
he'd fucking win. First saw him urinate
against *Beach Side Gallery*'s door, frown,
perambulate
                as if that girl waiting for his finish
was nothing, or nothing's memory. Diminished
he yells: 'Screw it, it's pissing over.'
She ties hair - Warm winds skim ex-lover's
words. No tears.

He spies a couple, fears
swearing before their baby son.
'Sorry, cursing in front of the kiddie,
didn't hear it, mate, did he?'
'No worries, he's heard worse.'
Somehow, the whole beach knows that's a lie.

Red killer-wedges
skittering ahead
she takes the lead,
skinny legs edge holidaymakers.
Siren lips breathe:
'Too right it's over, loser.'
Hitching black micro-skirt
fumbles crimson belt,
scarlet nails scrape emerging mobile.
He gobs words at her:
'You behaved bleedin' vile!'

She watches him go. No
hint of chasing after
and, you suspect, his tears'll
soon cause laughter.

Pumped lips air-kiss the mobile:
'The King is dead.'
(*Jackie O* shades repeat his shrinking frame)

'Understand. Not playing some weird game,
I meant it when I said that other thing -
But did you get it, Roy? We just came back from burying the King.'

Let's Not Stick Around for This

If I were that thin bloke, shunting my *Volvo* into
her Pimp-Mobile, I'd do *Chariots of Fire*
down the Prom.

Arms pumped into aqua trackie,
breasts ballooning righteous anger,
coming for him, vampire sniffing blood,
no one (this side of sanity) would
hang round to see
grief she's
        going to visit
                on his puny body.

Silver… Orange headlights
wind neon-chains around her neck.
On-coming train wreck,
(bloody hell, she's wearing knuckle-dusters!)
and doubts, any doubts,
she's going to hurt him – look –
her eyes –
silver bullets to his cringing werewolf,
lips spout water,
he's the West's Wicked Witch,
or drinking bourbon in *The Last Chance Saloon*
drawing spades as, outside, his horse bolts.
Doubt, any doubt, she's going to work him over,
look – Her lions roar his gladiatorial name,
she's the pin-up astride a pointy bomb,
he's an unmade mobster, entering the wrong
garage on Saint Valentine's.

She don't need life coaches, Germaine Greer …
Uri Gellar… Paul McKenna…
Don't need God on her side,
money banked, unconditional love to bring this down.
'Let's talk about it', isn't on the cards.
Torso-ripples spit: 'We're hard… Hard… HARD…'

Unless he can fly like Superman,
owns cloaks of invisibility,
is white Mohammed Ali
masquerading as a nerd,
he's had it. Screwed,
life spat out and chewed.

Let's not stick around for this ugly moment in the buzzing night,
death's no spectator sport, it isn't right.

Escapologists

I

Police sirens drown her white heeled
struggle past bald-faced hotels, past
Stags and fuchsia-tinted Hens: 'L' plates, midriffs
lit by belly rings. Case wheeled
through carnivorous laughter.
Her blank stare lost among plastic veils,
and 'kiss-me-quick', among promises
scattered as do-nut sprinkles.
Couples barge to *Bar de la Mer*,
she joins the cab queue,
whole life in a wheelie-case.

Suppose a song on the radio lyricised what you knew?
Song slicing breakfast, elegantly blue:
'Run away...
act today,...
get gone...
that song can't be wrong...'

II

Today the day. Quit the hotel as if strolling,
inner child warning 'run', but no, walk -
Good suit. Polished brogues. Hair teased. Tie straight.
Leave staff stuff you've failed to relocate
(plus false address, bad credit,
non-existent number).
'Can I speak to Mr Chaworth, please? He doesn't? Really?'
(Bloody great!)

His time to walk away... get gone... escape with that song...

III

I legged it. Unsure why.
Perhaps open doors crackled invitation.
Perhaps it was a song,
there are better and worse reasons,
though nothing in my life seemed out of place… wrong,
it felt for ages like I'd mislaid something.
Walked. Now sit in this hotel
staring at sea through nauseous curtains.
Then picture you
opening emptied wardrobes,
coat-hangers' rattle-dance
echoing: 'Why?'
What can I say?
Song on the radio whispered: 'This could be you',
soft voice over cornflakes, bolt out of the blue:
'Walk away… get gone… that song isn't wrong'

Regent

Ghosting the Pavilion, struggling to catch your eye
as you study pock-marked mirrors I knew new.
Shock of my floury, moon-pie
face, hair seeming too small and not well curled,
spirit of better times, bereft of dogs… parties… mistresses…

Hoping to make tourists, like yourself, recoil
my impressive form's refracted
in one hundred
knives…   forks…   spoons…
Shudders in and out of compotes
hefty with wax fruit, whorls eyes
of porcelain Mandarins
                             to no effect.

Through Gift Shop shelves I squish,
tinkling pot-bellied Christmas baubles,
juddering gewgaws, rattling shrink-wrapped postcards
(depicting regal under-drawers that can't be mine
too large, sink me, too large)
and think of breathing times
when trifling debts were trumpeted
around the house, and penny-sheets lampooned me
fat enough to sport those mighty under-drawers.

Listen. Sore phantom feet squelched
into silk Chinese slippers for eternity
task your steps. I call… call…
nothing sounds against empty air…

Outside, exotic borders roaring with a thousand scarlet Dragon-tongues.

Jimmy and Steph

That couple on The Pier,
Jimmy and Steph from *Quadrophenia*,
grown up, grown old, back here
for an all-nighter. Enquires how she's been,
hears of grand-kids, Hubby's shed,
anything, except some nights
she hears his scooter pass by Mum and Dads'
hairdryer hum intact. He chats
of ex-wives, ex-jobs, new Time-Share
(still digs back-combed hair
and streamlined skirts), passing *Rock Shop*
lists past Faces who'll attend the gig and,
laughing as some fat bloke munches sugar fried-eggs,
takes her hand …
                She remembers snaps of them
are back at the hotel, show him later, lets things stand,
he feels her wedding-ring upbraid hard skin,
marvels she doesn't let him go
as, sharing natter from *Mod-Net*
discovers who's in trouble, broke, or dead.
Thinks him unchanged, just chrome-shot hair,
can still look good in *Slim Fits*.
Who'd've twigged they'd date Brighton again,
if only for a weekend?
In her head, unutterable: 'Stay,
let's not go back', they'll never say.
Cases re-strapped, re-donned beige and grey,
the *S-t-a P-r-e-s-t* black and blue of yesterday.

Permanent Crease

Clothes too pinched, worn after better times,
dance-hall doors close, in his mind,
parked scooters slump and burn.
Wish-bone ankles connecting *Hipsters* ... socks,
Fine Poynts slop,
size nines shield size six feet.
Hovers *Jump the Gun*
asks: 'When're *The Who* playing?'
Emptied gaze straying
over my figure (wish
I stood more distant).

'Sunday', says the assistant.
'Sunday?'
'Sunday.'
'Tickets, are there?'
'Yeah.'
'Tickets?'
'YES, THERE ARE.'
'Tickets.'
Stone-wash irises glance again,
collecting rain
under shrunk leather *Porkpie* -
bootlace curls in need of care.
Stare:
'Wonder who'll be there?
Won't recognise me now,
old 'in-crowd'.
Still. Sunday.'

Face more pressed than his *Crombie*,
its glue of badges: Target, *Long
Tall Shorty,
Start! Come
Dancing, The One,
Small Faces* ...

Before he's done, before the long
hot summer swallows his small face
he flashes one
last look, then gone.

We Are (Still) the Mods:
Mod – Modernist, moderniser

        Along The Front, passing *The Grand, The Regency
        Ramada* (old *Hotel Norfolk*), hum chromic wasps.
        Targets, bull's-eyes … Multi-mirrors
        refract ice-cream parlours
        dripping with liquorice bikers,
        harassed dads, *Barbie*-pink wands,
        rock-willies gripped in leatherette hands,
        Daiquiri-and-Lime haired grans.
        Carnaby carnival.
        Buzzing along, unexpected pillions –
       Behind *The Who*'s Jimmy and Steph
      ace faces – Charley Hawtrey, Kenny Williams,
     spindly legs, open mouths guffaw
    toward *W.C. Boggs'* staff shindig,
   stuffed pockets roar
  with fluffy lions, won on a Pier that's derelict again,
 band strumming *Back Where We Started*
through fine-etched English rain.

From *Dome* or *Pleasure Gardens*
  previous modernists bum lifts,
    Rex Whistler
              op-art helmet, shades, matched hipsters,
       Max Miller
            flora-dora coat and trilby,
              single entendre confetti
                 showered over plump-legged sirens,
                      oceanic curls bobby-pinned
           Pinkie's chinned
       a weedy bloke into
     taking him to
    Brighton Races,
   whirring faces
  become razors …

and does a *Vespa* exist broad
  enough to cushion
   blue-blood buttocks?
     Chinese bells percussion
      thunder thighs. Regent arms caress
       driver's mermaid breasts,
         she, aware her shaking pillion
          sighs, fretting to leave
             white fairy-cake Pavilion.

Dandies

Self Portrait of the Artist as Tank Commander

i.m. Rex Whistler, 1905-1944

Insouciant, I'd appear at home, these days, in Brighton.
Savouring L*emon Drop Martini*,
or sauntering *The Grand*. If still around
would whistle along with *The Divine Comedy*
(*Victory for the Comic Muse* my album, darlings).

Consider, in shadow I've Mod flair,
starched shirt, razored hair,
manicure, elegant legs
reflected in patent boots, bum-
caresser jacket accentuating slender rear.

Brass buttons imply darker missions,
bunched brushes placed aside,
wine glass poised for putting down,
unlikeliest town gunslinger, prepared to ride
into tequila sunrise.

Re-fashioned self within
blue-sky metropolitan
terraces. Slant lips
imply to revellers: 'This could be it.'
(Despite claimed celebration

of fresh-unpacked identity) lounge lizard
turned chameleon, blushing khaki,
triumph of fancy – new dress, new uniformity.

Cool irony, the model officer I proved to be …
Definitely the Comic Muse's brittle victory.

The Boy with Harold Steptoe's Despair

Inside, feels himself intended for a better-class of ride,
than terraces where class-mates sniggered: 'Look at him,
thinks he's summat!'
Knows he can get the girl, but bringing her back through doors
shamed with someone else's graffiti won't make her stay
(times he's painted over *Nottingham Massive in the Hood*
the boggers always spray it back).

Dreams he's some effortlessly languid
playboy – laundered shirt, dice-links,
tie-pin starry as witticisms breathed
over a *Metropolitan*, which seduce
orchidaceous women on ocean liners,
just far enough from shore
for bed to be a sure-
fire bet.
      He's woken by milk vans' shushing,
yards below baptised by drunks pissing.
Getting up to interrogate the mirror, sees
not the sharp dressed man's rising mercury
but bleary frustrations of a T.V. ragman's son
dreaming an Aston Martin as his cart
jolts through streets in black and white.

'Let Me Tell You the Story of My Life ...'

he said: 'It's raining out there, and we're both stuck,
might pass an odd hour,' he coughed, passing thin hands
through age-bleached hair. 'Lived in Soho, just after the war,
and later, rum lot we were, used to go to ...
What was it blasted called? *The Colony Room*!
Landlady looked a bit like you. Met Francis Bacon
once, though didn't know, till after, what he did.
And, in the Fifties, met... what was her name?
Film star... blonde... big breasts... sorry, but they were ...
No, it's passed me by! She was quite lovely, though,'
aqua eyes glimmer under folded lids,
'mixed crowd – painters, poets, ex-service, the odd
actor, always on edge it seemed to me, Diana Dors!
That was that woman! Knew I'd get there.
Dylan Thomas once spilled a pint over my brogues,
was it him? Or that drunken painter? Minton? Minter? Rogue
fellow, used to have Casino jaunts with him ...
another time saw that film-actress, lovely,
luminous blonde, what was her name?
No, don't say it, it'll come to me, love, always does,
in that black dress, you look a bit like a club landlady I once knew,
                    now, let me tell you ...

Teds and Aristos

'I am consumed with curiosity to know where the Teddy Boys find the money to indulge their rather nostalgic taste for Edwardian dress.'
(Lady Child, Cobham Park House, Surrey, in *The Daily Express*, 1954)

for M.B.

Hard Boys. Razor Kings. Dukes of Earl.
Bad Bad Lads. Hate and hate on white knuckles,
and they all had to be borstal-fodder,
hooligans, yahoos... flick-knife grins
and rebel shine making girls want them.
Razor Kings. Dukes of Earl.
'Come on pretty baby, guess where we got cash
to indulge Flash
         Harry nostalgia?'

Razor Boys. Kings of Earl. Hard Lads.
Drainpipes, velour collars, playing being
Edwardians, putting on the style
but not the agony of futures
facing trench and dugout.
Hard boys ... Dukes of Earl
on HP.
Who do they think they might be?
Brothel-creepers, crepes and drapes
hidden from sepia parents
acid blues and pinks peeking
like burlesque girls from
         behind wardrobes.

Being Flash Harriet myself, chiselled tones dog
heels down mirrored corridors I don't belong in.
When introduced, my flick-knife smile
makes them ask where I found the bottle
to flare Fifties-kitsch in tasteful faces –
like frilly knickers, skull-earrings,
polka-dotted underskirts, meant, they fear,
to be eyed-up by rabble-rousing hard boys, razor kings,
         and Dukes of Earl.

Good Time Girl II: Vanitini

Back-street Casanova, Alfie pushing sixty,
Rank charms make wanting him sensible
as shagging for virginity
but women entertain him as a form of light relief
though their inner Mary Whitehouse nags he's probably a thief.

He's just a *Metropolitan Mandritini*
flirting with the next disaster,
eyes behind Mod shades
iced as a *Raff Slammer*.

He's sipping *Dame Shamer*,
Esquire Martini, Bosom for a Pillow,
but, funnily enough, *Reform*'s not on the menu.
Still … ladettes entertain him as a form of light relief
though their inner Julie Andrews sings he's probably a thief.

Straight from a town called Malice
to a wine bar on your list
and you shouldn't drop your cover
just because you're slightly pissed.

His B-movie Casanova maintaining rumpled charm
suggests maybe there are worse fates
than being on his arm.
I'm not first to recognise him as a form of light relief,
though my inner Christine Keeler pleads he's probably a thief.

River Song

Earl of Rochester's ghost stalks moody
by the Thames tonight,
rake-hell sun quick setting,
spilling tallow light,
and he passes softly through us
as if we're not all there,
river breezes sighing through silk hair.

The Earl of Rochester's spectre misremembers
that last whore,
can't recollect her face
recalls a slamming door,
tender billowed sleeves
fill with October's chill,
as he wonders if she's waiting for him still …

joins a Saraband
of once-were-libertines,
cold movers and dead shakers,
pox-patched might have beens,
dandinis, foppish dreamers,
maskers with a past,
and wonders why it is
sensation never lasts?

Earl of Rochester's shade stands
single once again,
entering a bar,
neon flickering like rain,
catch him staring through me
as if I wasn't there,
as though the hand of an old love was
tousling his hair…
                      neon's returned to normal,
as he's by the Thames again,
(sense him glancing backwards,
as if in sudden pain)

perhaps his grave's been stomped on,
made him suddenly aware,
slight as river mist
he'll just evaporate on air,
and once angels and once demons
might sink to rest at last,
on the sequinned river surface
and consign all to the past,
yet, as if she sat beside me
I'm suddenly aware,
of his last whore
gently whispering a prayer …

Links

Threaded tight by bronzed fingers,
paste, pearls, cubic-zirconia.
Aspirant P Diddys bling with logos –
become expensive corporation sandwich-men.

Holiday shirts 'carry on' with crumpet,
cheesecake, pin-ups, Sid and Babs,
Bettie Page,
Bogie and Bacall,
and the Rat Pack better be there, 'Pally.'

Sparking shirts of boys most likely to,
gangsta rap wanabees, diamond geezers from
Fitzgerald with love,
links crafted out of human molars.
Let's not go there, in case they ask what
WE THINK WE'RE LOOKING AT?

Stags and does,
ducks and drakes,
hens and cocks.

Grandad pulling links through initialled sleeves,
studs glimmering fragile wrists of croupiers, gamblers,
dodgers, pan-handlers,
long and short cons, snake oil sellers,
businessmen with Peter Sellers'
glasses, legit looking cases, uncensored eyes, cuffs

sporting *Asprey, Garrard, Cartier,*
nothing banked but bad, red debts,
and it doesn't matter if it's all a shot of dazzle,
all a bit of 'something for the weekend' fluff,
who's looking hard enough,
who gives a stuff
if they're *Asprey*
or Reg Asprey,
Portobello?

Monsieur Worth

When the Boss said 'him', I was sure he'd got it wrong,
wasn't 'he' our smart customer? Suit polite,
vowels well turned-out. Cuff-links, nacre tie-
pin against starch, face recalling Walter Matthau's.
Brylcreemed coaly hair razored into red nape,
hands manicured. Winter camel-coat scented with
Monsieur Worth, citrus insinuating round tills used
to *Brut, Fresh Knight,* or something worse.

Saturday's queue – sad smile hinting coming rejection.

'Don't sell it him, no matter how he looks, or what's said,
we all know what happens next.'
'Him, Boss, you sure?'
'Yeah', Roberta chimed, 'he doesn't look the type, but then,
I was a nurse, they never do.'

One slack afternoon, the new girl sold it him

before the Boss could give sufficient warning.
Our smartest customer left the shop,
just as my lunch-break started,
I saw him in the alley
by the chippie

left hand against the wall,
white nails gleaming,
right hand clutching
bottled lighter-fuel
he was swigging from.
Our eyes met, shoulders shrugged,
there went that too
sad smile again

saying: 'I know. There's nothing I can do'.

Dan Dare and the Mansfield Aliens

Floral shirt, striped strides, handkerchief, no tie,
faux name, Dan Dare, silk monogrammed underwear,
Italian jobbing winkle-pickers, scarf like women's frilly knickers,
publishing youth magazines, don't believe in modesty,
streaky bouffant blow dried, never seeming tongue tied,
manicure, aftershave, gets mistook for Michael Caine,
isn't going to get a wife, 'lived in London all his life.'
Sassoon … Carnaby, shop to make the world free,
dolly-mixture tinted plaid, always walking in the shade,
dark lenses sober Chelsea vista, never answering his sister's
calls, dreads visitations, cuts her from his swinging nation,
cotton dress so home made, prefers lemonade
to champagne any day, says she just came out that way:
'IN MANSFIELD' (let him mock, but it runs through her like rock
and she knows that he's ashamed: 'won't visit our Mother's grave,
impersonates a Londoner, doesn't know his nearest neighbour,
'birds' come, 'birds' gone, doesn't stick with one for long').
In that bit before it's light, bitter words are dynamite,
come the middle of the night, even he suspects she's right.
Glad to put her on the bus, nothing further to discuss.

Convene, so hip, buy at *Granny Takes A Trip*,
be *Lord Kitchener's Valet*, dandified and glad to say
he celebrates his inner Dare, loves the way old women stare.
Behind his hankie, paper poke from a knackered envelope,
legacy contained inside, only removed when she died,
thinning band of hollow-tin, Mother's tarnished wedding ring.

Dan Dare's Living Daylights

Sees himself reflected in their shades but not their eyes,
funfair mirror moment with ladies from Shanghai,
happy they're on his arm, more relaxed alone,
vaguely wonders where his weekend's gone.
One to replace another, a briefer, lighter fling,
seems they're getting younger, but don't penetrate his skin …
Some day comes acknowledgment, as outer-doors get slammed,
maybe this is getting out of hand.

Still, practised moves and chatter at the disco when he's tight,
swears he'll fall in love but, somehow, never plays that right,
as minis become maxis and kaftans turn to flairs,
less of them negotiate his stairs.

Enter loud Sloane Rangers (he has a few of those)
adopting an *Armani* suit and classic business pose,
too soon decades are melting, future almost there,
he finds school-leavers tinting his grey hair.

Still, reveres bright cocktails, sanctifies weekends,
returns to swinging schmutter, rejecting sporty trends,
rogue girls enjoy his chat-up, though now seldom takes one home,
relieved to buy them *Taboo*, happiest alone,
and he's loping down the seafront, towards another night,
face fired chrome and crimson (unforgiving neon light)
seems just seconds later he's fumbling at the door
for keys impressed against sharp hips a few seconds before …

and I see him at the Café, as tonged hair won't take the rain,
or cavorting with a hen night, then breezing out again,
find him at the bar, buying leery girls a drink,
as he's striding by me, gives a little wink.
Sees himself reflected in my shades but not my eyes,
and he's waiting on tomorrow, for tomorrow never dies.

Dan Dare and the Vanished Years

He's wearing Brighton-Rock
stripe trousers, no, not trousers, strides.
                                    Flock-
wallpaper shirt, hibiscus silk
cravat, and mood-indigo shades.
Sunlight makes
skin crawl (makes
him feel light, fading snap
of someone who once lived here)
and hurts his eyes.
Blending with *Novelty Shop* flower-power
chatter washes over as the girl sighs:
'Can I help you, love?'

He steps away …
Club flyers skitter the Prom, young men
impersonate his former selves,
pink and baby-blue posters promote
Shangri-La Lounge, Hung on You, drag
queens doing Dusty, *The Honey Club*
where mini-skirted dollies sport.
Winds mess with sculpted hair
as he heads for *The Regency*'s espresso,
shirt and strides clashing with
barely observed seascapes.
Sometimes, an old bird's recognition makes
him act as if her face's unrecalled,
mumbling goodbyes through pursing lips,
as, cigarette in hand,
he steps away.

Velvet suited nights await,
too much Merlot,
and hasty confidences
instantly withdrawn.

Step away, last Harlequin, keeping pictures
from the past on ice – the glimmered disco-ball,
op-art mini, bunch of aquamarine-
paper daisies, already drooping
on velour-coated stems.

Montague Burton: Most Definitely a Ladies' Man

They don't know what I'm thinking, and by the time they've
clicked, I'll be moved on to the next hotel,
the *Esplanade* or *Grand*. When *These Foolish Things* is played
they'll think of me, and I of them, but not in the same way.

I stand immaculate – from the board-room-table polish of my shoes,
to nacre cufflinks (how they appreciate a man who manicures,
confiding 'my Gerald never manicures,'
and isn't it all about confidences, when push comes to elegant shove?)

I used to love this game, the ins and outs, and irate husbands,
chances to be a Count, vagabond film star, beloved infidel,
but now it seems a whipper-snapper's pursuit,
I tire of acting somebody.

Sparking bar-mirrors repeat my ruined face,
still handsome in a folded sort of way, and see
lost women circle, their rounds predictable
and glowing blank as pearlised buttons on a well-starched shirt.

Bread and Cakes

'The Rookeries', Ghent - *Bloch Freres* Patisserie,
'don't enter for fast food', warn past clients etched
on wall-friezes. Slightly peeling tables
reassuring as tea-dances.

Four waitresses take sweet time.

Interlaced buns, *Passover Matzos*,
cinnamon dusted apple-strudel,
naked pastry Eves and Adams
press cherry-noses on windows.
Heath-Robinson urns, espresso steam
mean my fogged eyes ignore
old gent juggling books and stick, shadowing doors.

Mist cleared, I let him in. 'Merci. I pay
you drink for that?' 'It's fine', I say.
Taking my hand in manicured fingers,
he smiles, re-arranges books,
makes known another stick.

Gingerbread patisserie Flaneur
bows, strides
to the Café's baking heart.

Filtering coffee ticks,
fondant-cupids served to glamorous old
women as, outside, disputing couples barge.

What of family Bloch in occupation?
Hard to picture times when windows crammed with
shortbread witches, saints, serving men, didn't ice
The Rookeries' plain cake.

Lost confection,
built back sheaf on fragile plaited sheaf?

Risen immaculate
as elegant monsieur balanced by sticks.

No Man

'I'm the Urban Spaceman, Baby, here comes the twist, I don't exist.'
(The Bonzos)

i.m. Vivian Stanshall

Midge marked by bosky-fingered 'No Man's Heath',
Dad pulls into a lay-by, windscreen bleared.
Late August's Hawkweed – scattered Hydra teeth,
glimpsed bushes seem hung fleeces, freshly sheared.
Car bored, 'I Spy', a geezer with flame beard,
haunting the heath in full Victorian dress –
cape shifting as if spectral tourists cleared.
Grave dinner-suit – silk waistcoat sprigged with cress,
He lumbers clear-felled brash as light grows less.

I'm nine, don't call this serendipity
(warm against window-glass, my thumb ends press,
trace 'havershambling' eccentricity).

Dead or not, some ghosts impress odd regions,
like re-enactors playing Roman legions.

Regular

About that linear cigarette
held within porcelain fingers. The
cane twirled under the other palm. He
gazes, pupils shaded rivers, and yet
sees no one, ballads swim with regret,
misting the bar, his cane raps. Suddenly
mirrors holding men he used to be.
Acknowledged? No, better to forget …
Black suit, jet tie, shirt crisp, gloss shoes,
crimson socks, red handkerchief. Poised
listlessly, addresses barmaids: 'Darling.'
Soft lips telling familiar blues
as eyes scan walls, espresso voice,
perched cane, glanced moment, stalling.

Portrait of Mr...

All time-traveller,
Belle Époque flaneur,
fetched-up in century where
he'll never hear slushed carriage-wheels again,
alone at bars, pre-sentenced aesthete
dock bound eyes commanding rain.

I want to paint him.

Seen three times, three days. Same
pristine cashmere ...
Hued for parakeets,
dandy's carnation,
Emerald City skyscraper.

Once, *boulevardier*,
stylish limp, silver-knobbed cane,
second in *Bar Medusa*, cane
spanning stools.
                 Last, ruled
by buoyant men, swayed in heavy laughter,
kind eyes focussing after
                softer faces.
Feather-cut dyed inky, framing mapped skin.

(Still love to paint him.)

Smiling past friends on promises,
men of certain age,
unlike him, all predatory.

Hang-on! Re-wind. Wait,
they're predatory, thumb-nailed
in pink and ochre paint?
Verdance singly haunting,
Lautrec's lost fop, stalking,
opening wardrobes where reside

pale shirts and strides,
layered beside -
rows of parakeet, Oz urbane,
fore-grounded green
carnation sweaters meaning -

Our man's noted, singled out,
nothing worse, quips Oscar,
than not being talked about.

Flaneur

Kagool sheathed, they rush, avoiding rain,
crushing past awnings' gushing waterfalls
and there he's cloistered. Elegance calls
attention (world's washed down a drain).
Dove-grey suit, with silver-headed cane,
exotic plant against Plain Jane pub walls
and, for an instant, sodden summer stalls,
pub front transformed to sudden picture-frame.

Could be imagining yellow rose,
tonal handkerchief, glossed ballroom shoes,
my nocturne formed of brushstrokes and regret,
torch song from a vanquished Pierrot Show.

He's real enough. Discussing current news.
Blue smoke furling from his cigarette.

Notes

Greene-land
All these characters first appeared in Graham Greene's *Brighton Rock* (1938); Greene's *A Gun For Sale* was published in 1936.

The Brighton Mystery
The title of a 1924 film, for all film references see: Frank Grey et al, *Kiss and Kill: Film Visions of Brighton* (2002).

Under Suspicion
1991 film set in Brighton.

Good Time Girl
1948 film set in Brighton.

Time at the Patrick Hamilton
Withnail and I (1987); for a life of Patrick Hamilton see Nigel Jones, *Through A Glass Darkly* (1991).

Heist
Frank Miller's graphic-novel series (also a 2005 film) featured many dames worth dying for, described in language straight from Chandler and Hammett.

Escapologists
After Ray Davies's 2006 song 'Lonesome Train' on *Other People's Lives* (2006).

Self Portrait of the Artist as Tank Commander
Inspired by the exhibition, *Rex Whistler the Triumph of Fancy*, curated by Stephen Calloway at the Brighton Museum and Art Gallery, 2006.

The Boy With Harold Steptoe's Despair
After Ray Davies's 'Celluloid Heroes' (*The Kinks Greatest Celluloid Heroes*, 2001).

Teds and Aristos
See Dominick Sandbrook, *Never Had It So Good*: 1956-1963 (2005)

Good Time Girl II: Vanitini
The names italicised or in bold are cocktails.

No Man
'Havershambling' was *The Bonzos* frontman, Vivian Stanshall's, word. 'Urban Spaceman' (1969) can be found on *The History of the Bonzos* (1997).